I Want to Be an Engineer

Written by Peter J

This book belongs to

_ _ _ _ _ _ _ _ _ _ _ _ _ _ _ _ _ _

I want to be an engineer when I grow up. Engineers build things and solve problems. I think it would be fun to design and create things that help people.

I like to build things with Lego. I make cars, planes, and houses. I also like to take things apart to see how they work. Then I try to put them back together again.

At school I really enjoy my math and science classes. Engineers use math and science every day when they are designing things. They test different ideas to find solutions.

There are many different types of engineers. Some work on cars or airplanes. Others build bridges, roads, and tall buildings. Software engineers create computer programs and apps.

I read books about engineering to learn more. My parents gave me fun building toy sets for my birthday too. I practice drawing designs and schematics for things I want to build someday.

Last week we toured a construction site downtown to see the giant cranes and equipment being used. We all wore hard hats to stay safe. It was cool to see engineering in action!

When I go to college I will study subjects like engineering, math, and physics to become an engineer. I will get to work in a job where I can design, create, and solve important problems.

As an engineer I want to invent new technologies that make people's lives easier. Maybe I could design faster computers or better robots. I have so many ideas to contribute!

I know engineering will be challenging but also very rewarding. I can't wait to build prototypes in a workshop. And it will be exciting when my designs are manufactured to help real people.

Becoming an engineer takes hard work and dedication but it's what I really dream of doing. With creativity and persistence, I know I can utilize my love of science and math in this career someday!

I like to volunteer doing activities related to engineering. Last month I helped judge my school's science fair and saw many cool experiments. Maybe I could design an experiment to test materials and strengths.

Over the summer my uncle said I could job shadow him at the tech company where he works. He is a software engineer who designs apps and computer programs. I can't wait to see him code something new!

In the future I want to find ways to make the world cleaner and greener. As an engineer I could invent better solar panels, electric cars, or energy-efficient devices. Helping the environment is very important to me.

There are so many incredible things that engineers get to work on and create. Bridges, spacecrafts, medical devices – the list is endless! With dedication I can do this too and shape the future.

Here's what I need to do:

- In high school and college, I'll take hard math and science classes. They help me become a great engineer.

-Engineers are curious and keep trying until they solve problems.

-I'll learn cool skills like drawing, using design programs, building things, coding, and playing with robots.

-Being creative is super important. I get to think of new ideas that no one thought of before!

-Teamwork is fun. Engineers work together and share their cool ideas.

-I'll pay close attention to details. Even small things matter.

-Engineering always changes. I'll keep learning new things.

-I love solving tough problems. It's like a cool challenge.

-After college, I'll get a special degree in engineering. That's where I learn lots of awesome stuff.

-I'll do internships, like a sneak peek into the engineering world.

-I'll find what I love, like helping people, designing bridges, or making clean energy.

-I'll keep learning even after college. There's always something new in engineering.

-Engineers want to make the world better, like creating better healthcare or cool bridges.

-If I work hard in math, science, and being creative, I can be an awesome engineer too!

I'm going to start preparing now by studying hard and learning all I can. If I keep my creativity sparked and never give up, someday I will get to achieve my dream of becoming an engineer!

Peter J wholeheartedly cheers on every child with dreams, urging them to follow their passions, and sincerely hopes that their dreams come true. If you enjoy Peter J's book, we would truly appreciate your feedback in the form of a review and a star rating. Your thoughts and ratings mean a lot, as Peter J is committed to creating even more enjoyable books for your reading delight. Thank you wholeheartedly for your ongoing support.

By the same author: Peter J
Already published: